BOOK OF PUTIN
WORDS THAT CHANGE THE WORLD

Introduction

This collection, edited by Set, a Russian youth political movement, was originally published as a holiday gift to a select group of Russian officials -- MPs, regional governors and civil society representatives. An accompanying letter explained that the book should be seen as a guide to the Kremlin's "values and guiding principles" and "required reading for any politician."

This book is an English language translation of the original. It includes quotes drawn from the past 12 years of Mr. Putin's most important speeches and interviews, and highlights key quotes that is said to have "predicted and preordained" world events. The editors hoped Russian officials would use the book as "a manual for action, for understanding."

The manifesto of Set (which in Russian means both "Network" and "Fishing Net") describes it as a group of young people who believe Putin is a collective father figure for Russians. It says: "We are together with the father, at one with him. We do not fight against the power of the father; we share it, we learn to use it, and together with the father we direct its energy towards our present and future."

The movement's Moscow office recruits creative young people to produce stirring patriotic products with a hint of style about them. To enroll, members simply need to provide a positive answer to the key question: "Are you for Putin?"

If you aspire to be a leader of your own country, you must speak your own language, for God's sake.

The biggest nationalist in Russia — that's me.
Russia is my whole life.

Sometimes it is necessary to be lonely in order to prove that you are right.

It's clear that from 1924 to 1953, the country led by Stalin changed fundamentally; industrialization certainly did take place. We won the Great Patriotic War. And whatever anyone may say, victory was achieved. Even when we consider the losses, no one now can throw stones at those who planned and led this victory.

We should acknowledge that the collapse of the Soviet Union was a major geopolitical disaster of the century.

Whoever does not miss the Soviet Union has no heart. Whoever wants it back has no brain.

The path towards a free society has not been simple. There are tragic and glorious pages in our history.

We need to develop respect for our history, despite all of its flaws, and love for the Motherland. We need to pay the utmost attention to our common moral values and consolidate Russian society on this basis. I think that this is an absolute priority.

Russia is an ancient country with historical, profound traditions and a very powerful moral foundation. And this foundation is a love for the Motherland and patriotism. Patriotism in the best sense of that word. Incidentally, I think that to a certain extent, to a significant extent, this is also attributable to the American people.

Russia has made its choice in favor of democracy. Fourteen years ago, independently, without any pressure from outside, it made that decision in the interests of itself and interests of its people, of its citizens. This is our final choice, and we have no way back. There can be no return to what we used to have before.

We will not allow the past to drag us down and stop us from moving ahead.

I was just a boy when I started judo. I became deeply interested in martial arts, their special philosophy, culture, relations with the opponent and the rules of combat.

Judo is not just a sport. It's a philosophy. And it's not for weaklings.

Only one thing works: Go on the offensive. You must hit first, and hit so hard that your opponent will not rise to his feet.

At one point I really wanted to be a pilot.
But then books and spy movies took hold of my
imagination. I saw how one man's effort could
achieve what whole armies could not. From
then on I wanted to be a spy.

My notion of the KGB came from romantic spy stories. I was a pure and utterly successful product of Soviet patriotic education.

There is no such thing as a former KGB man.

Spying has always gone on since ancient times.

When I was young I didn't try to command people. It was more important to preserve my independence. If I had to compare it with my adult life, I would say that the role I played as a kid was like the role of the judicial branch, and not the executive.

I just love everything new. I enjoy learning new things. The process itself gives me great pleasure.

I drink kefir.

I don't read books by people who have betrayed the Motherland.

I have a private life in which I do not permit interference. It must be respected. Nobody should ever interfere in others' private lives. I have always reacted negatively to those who, with their snotty noses and erotic fantasies, prowl into others' lives.

I like all Russian women. I personally think Russian women are the most talented and beautiful.

The more I know about people, the more I like dogs. Dogs and I have very warm feelings for one another.

I am the wealthiest man, not just in Europe, but in the whole world. I collect emotions.

At least the state figure should have a head.

One should never fear threats. It's like with a dog. A dog senses when somebody is afraid of it, and bites. The same applies with humans. If you become jittery, they will think that they are stronger.

Russia – we – are constantly being taught about democracy. But for some reason, those who teach us do not want to learn themselves. That is plunging the world into an abyss of permanent conflicts. This is extremely dangerous. No one feels safe

If you press the spring too hard it will snap back. You must always remember this.

If a person is satisfied with everything, he is a
complete idiot. A normal person cannot be
satisfied with everything.

I've a feeling I'll get everything I want.

The Comrade Wolf knows whom to eat, as the saying goes. It knows whom to eat and is not about to listen to anyone, it seems.

Sometimes it's better to act faster doing mistakes than do nothing at all.

No one should be allowed to violently trample on the law. You must obey the law, always, not only when they grab you by your special place.

Thieves must sit in prison.

You can swim any way you like... in the Dead Sea.

True sovereignty is an absolute necessity for Russia's existence.

Being isolationist or xenophobic is weak.
We are strong and believe in ourselves.

We in Russia turn a sports competition into a really spectacular event and we are good at it.

We don't need a weakened government but a strong government that would take responsibility for the rights of the individual and care for the society as a whole.

Territorial integrity of Russia can't be compromised. We won't give in to threats and blackmail. We will employ all means — all legal means — at our disposal to quell those who dream of taking away any part of Russian territory.

The strengthening of our statehood is, at times, deliberately interpreted as authoritarianism.

Russia must realize its full potential in high-tech sectors such as modern energy technology, transport and communications, space and aircraft building.

There are both things in international law: the principle of territorial integrity and right to self-determination.

The fact that the union of different nationalities and denominations resulted from the liberation, this is particularly symbolic and important for our multinational country. As long as we feel this unity inside us, Russia will be invincible. Nobody and nothing will stop Russia on the road to strengthening democracy and ensuring human rights and freedoms.

I have a very positive attitude to anyone who is protecting the environment, but it's inadmissible when people are using it as a means of promoting themselves, using it as a source of self-enrichment. I don't want to name any specific examples, but often, environmentalism is used to blackmail companies.

The fact that the union of different nationalities and denominations resulted from the liberation, this is particularly symbolic and important for our multinational country. As long as we feel this unity inside us, Russia will be invincible.

In many countries today, moral and ethical norms are being reconsidered; national traditions, differences in nation and culture are being erased.

Let us resolve the internal political problems of Russia ourselves.

Political activities in Russia should be as transparent as possible. Financing political activities from abroad is something the state should keep an eye on.

We don't need a weakened government but a strong government that would take responsibility for the rights of the individual and care for the society as a whole.

Protest actions and propaganda are two
slightly different things.

Those who fight corruption should be clean themselves.

Some countries in the Middle East and North Africa, which used to be stable and relatively prosperous — Iraq, Libya, Syria — have turned into zones of chaos and anarchy that pose a threat to entire world. We know why it happened. We know who wanted to oust unwanted regimes, and rudely impose their own rules. They triggered hostilities, destroyed statehoods, set people against each other and simply washed their hands — giving way to radicals, extremists and terrorists.

We are facing a destructive barbaric ideology again and we have no right to allow those new obscurants to achieve their goals. We have to abandon all differences, create a single fist, a single anti-terrorist front, which would act in accordance with the international law and under the aegis of the United Nations.

I bow my head to the victims of terrorism.

Terrorism has no nationality or religion. I think the international community should unite to fight such inhuman phenomenon as terror attacks and the murder of totally innocent people.

Terrorists are always a threat to someone.
If we'll be scared of them, it means they have
won.

I am convinced that today terrorism poses the main threat to human rights and freedoms as well as to the sustainable development of states and people, We shall fight against terrorists, throw them in prison and destroy them.

We'll chase terrorists everywhere. If in an airport, then in the airport. If in the toilet, we'll waste them in the outhouse. Case closed.

Russia doesn't negotiate with terrorists.
It destroys them.

To forgive the terrorists is up to God, but to send them to Him is up to me.

If you want to become an Islamic fundamental-
ist and be circumcised, come to Moscow. We
are multiconfessional. We have very good
specialists. I can recommend one for the
operation. He'll make sure nothing grows back.

Any attention to them (terrorists) on the part of the media, any double-standard interpretation of their motives and results of their activity means nothing but a political and administrative support of terrorist acts.

My personal position is that society must keep children safe.

Sometimes it seems to me that certain European leaders want to be more Muslim that the Prophet Mohammad.

Everything will probably never be okay.
But we have to try for it.

The unjustified swelling of the budgetary deficit
and the accumulation of public debts are just as
destructive as adventurous stock-jobbing.

Hitler wanted to destroy Russia. Everyone needs to remember how that ended.

With these heroic events began the spiritual rebirth of the fatherland, the formation of a power great and sovereign.

Russians have different far lofty ambitions; more of a spiritual kind. It's more about your relationship with God.

Our aims are absolutely clear: They are a high living standard in the country and a secure, free and comfortable life.

Russia will not soon become, if it ever becomes,
a second copy of the United States or England –
where liberal value have deep historic roots.

I think the American people should express their preferences, and we'll accept their choice. President Obama hasn't been elected by the American people in order to be pleasant to Russia.

Primarily the United States has overstepped its national borders, and in every area. It's alarming that military intervention in internal conflicts in foreign countries has become commonplace for the United States.

Sometimes it's unclear whether to speak to a country's government or their US patrons.

Russia is a part of European culture. Therefore, it is with difficulty that I imagine NATO as an enemy.

The process of NATO expansion has nothing to do with modernization of the alliance. We have the right to ask, "Against whom is this expansion directed?"

.

Do we place our troops at US borders? Who is placing NATO troops, military infrastructure closer to us? Does anyone listen to us, talk to us about it? No, nothing. There is always the same response: it's not your business.

They won't leave the bear alone. They will always seek to chain it. And once it's chained, they'll rip out its teeth and claws.

There are no officials in my inner circle and I hope there will never be. I have colleagues. There are certain state functions that a man cannot perform once he gets personally close with people. I realized it long ago. I try to keep a certain distance from everyone, to work in a friendly atmosphere and with a full comprehension of the responsibility before the people.

One has to be insincere and promise something which you cannot fulfill. So you either have to be a fool who does not understand what you are promising, or deliberately be lying.

The motorcycle is the most democratic transport vehicle. It is the most daring, challenging as it gives its owner the tempting feeling of freedom, that is why one can say without any exaggeration, the bicycle is a symbol of freedom.

It is extremely dangerous to encourage people to see themselves as exceptional, whatever the motivation. There are big countries and small countries, rich and poor, those with long democratic traditions and those still finding their way to democracy. Their policies differ, too. We are all different, but when we ask for the Lord's blessings, we must not forget that God created us equal.

I have some rules of my own. One of them is never to regret anything. Over time, I came to the conclusion that this was the right thing to do. As soon as you start regretting and looking back, you start to sour. You always have to think about the future. You always have to look ahead. Of course you have to analyze your past mistakes, but only so that you can learn and correct the course of your life.

Russia needs a strong state power and must have it. But I am not calling for totalitarianism.

America's development began with a large-scale ethnic cleansing, unprecedented in human history.

History proves that all dictatorships, all authoritarian forms of government are transient. Only democratic systems are not transient. Whatever the shortcomings, mankind has not devised anything superior.

A country in which the people are not healthy physically and psychologically, are poorly educated and illiterate, will never rise to the peaks of world civilization."

Political activities in Russia should be as transparent as possible. Financing political activities from abroad is something the state should keep an eye on.

I am astonished that our internal law-making
is of such great interest to foreign governments.

Speaking of the sanctions, they are not just a knee-jerk reaction on behalf of the United States or its allies to our position regarding the events and the coup in Ukraine, or even the so-called Crimean Spring. I'm sure that if these events had never happened – I want to point this out specifically for you as politicians sitting in this auditorium – if none of that had ever happened, they would have come up with some other excuse to try to contain Russia's growing capabilities, affect our country in some way, or even take advantage of it.

I would like to speak about the most serious
and sensitive issue: international security. Since
2002, after the US unilaterally pulled out of the
ABM Treaty, which was absolutely a corner-
stone of international security, a strategic balance of forces and stability, the US has been
working relentlessly to create a global missile
defence system, including in Europe. This poses a
threat not only to Russia, but to the world as a
whole – precisely due to the possible disruption
of this strategic balance of forces.

It's difficult to talk to people who whisper even at home, afraid of Americans eavesdropping on them. It's not a figure of speech, not a joke, I'm serious.

The U.S. is a very democratic state. There's no doubt about that. And it originally developed as a democratic state. When the first settlers set their foot on the continent, life forced them to forge a relationship and maintain a dialogue with each other to survive. That's why America was conceived as a fundamental democracy.

It's not by chance that Russia and the U.S. forge alliances in the most critical moments of modern history. That was the case in WWI and WWII. Even if there was fierce confrontation, our countries united against a common threat, which means there's something that unites us. There must be some fundamental interest which brings us together. That's something we need to focus on first. We need to be aware of our differences but focus on a positive agenda that can improve our cooperation.

Russia does not have in its possession any trust-worthy data that supports the existence of nuclear weapons or any weapons of mass destruction in Iraq and we have not received any such information from our partners as yet.

Why don't you meet Osama bin Laden, invite him to Brussels or to the White House and engage in talks, ask him what he wants and give it to him so he leaves you in peace? You find it possible to set some limitations in your dealings with these bastards, so why should we talk to people who are child-killers? No one has a moral right to tell us to talk to child killers.

Russia has made its choice in favor of democracy. Fourteen years ago, independently, without any pressure from outside, it made that decision in the interests of itself and interests of its people — of its citizens. This is our final choice, and we have no way back. There can be no return to what we used to have before. And the guarantee for this is the choice of the Russian people, themselves. No, guarantees from outside cannot be provided. This is impossible. It would be impossible for Russia today. Any kind of turn towards totalitarianism for Russia would be impossible, due to the condition of the Russian society.

I see that not everyone in the West has understood that the Soviet Union has disappeared from the political map of the world and that a new country has emerged with new humanist and ideological principles at the foundation of its existence.

People in Russia say that those who do not regret the collapse of the Soviet Union have no heart, and those that do regret it have no brain. We do not regret this, we simply state the fact and know that we need to look ahead, not backwards. We will not allow the past to drag us down and stop us from moving ahead. We understand where we should move. But we must act based on a clear understanding of what happened.

I am not indifferent of course to the question of who will take in their hands the destiny of the country I have devoted my life to serving. But if each successive head of state were to change the Constitution to suit them, we would soon find ourselves without a state at all. I think that Russia's different political forces are sufficiently mature to realise their responsibility to the people of the Russian Federation. In any case, the person who receives the votes of the majority of Russian citizens will become the President of the country.

Not everyone likes the stable, gradual rise of our country. There are some who are using the democratic ideology to interfere in our internal affairs.

I will recall once more Russia's most recent history. Above all, we should acknowledge that the collapse of the Soviet Union was a major geopolitical disaster of the century. As for the Russian nation, it became a genuine drama. Tens of millions of our co-citizens and compatriots found themselves outside Russian territory. Moreover, the epidemic of disintegration infected Russia itself. Individual savings were depreciated, and old ideals destroyed. Many institutions were disbanded or reformed carelessly.

Many thought or seemed to think at the time that our young democracy was not a continuation of Russian statehood, but its ultimate collapse, the prolonged agony of the Soviet system. But they were mistaken. That was precisely the period when the significant developments took place in Russia. Our society was generating not only the energy of self-preservation, but also the will for a new and free life.

We have spoken on many occasions of the need to achieve high economic growth as an absolute priority for our country. The annual address for 2003 set for the first time the goal of doubling gross domestic product within a decade.

Russia must realize its full potential in high-tech sectors such as modern energy technology, transport and communications, space and aircraft building.

Russia does not want confrontation of any kind. And we will not take part in any kind of "holy alliance."

I stress that we unambiguously support strengthening the non-proliferation regime, without any exceptions, on the basis of international law.

A superpower is a cold war term. When people today say that Russia aspires to have this status, I interpret it in the following way: they want to undermine trust in Russia, to portray Russia as frightening, and create some kind of image of an enemy. Russia is in favor of a multipolar world, a democratic world order, strengthening the system of international law, and for developing a legal system in which any small country, even a very small country, can feel itself secure, as if behind a stone wall.

Russia is ready to become part of this multipolar world and guarantee that the international community observes these rules. And not as a superpower with special rights, but rather as an equal among equals.

If there is no possibility or, to put it in plain terms, if there is no money. What can you do? You can't go to a store, you can't buy anything, either a cannon, or a missile, or a medicine. For this reason the economy is at the basis of everything. In the beginning it was Karl Marx and then Freud and others.

We still have a great amount of work to do in social development, including resolving one of the biggest challenges we face in this area, namely, reducing the gap between high-income earners and people, citizens of our country, who are still living on very modest means indeed. But we cannot, of course, adopt the solution used 80 years ago and simply confiscate the riches of some to redistribute among others. We will use completely different means to resolve this problem, namely, we will ensure good economic growth.

The US defense budget in absolute figures is almost 25 times bigger than Russia's. This is what in defense is referred to as "their home – their fortress." And good for them, I say. Well done! But this means that we also need to build our home and make it strong and well protected. We see, after all, what is going on in the world.

I think there are things of which I and the people who have worked with me can feel deservedly proud. They include restoring Russia's territorial integrity, strengthening the state, progress towards establishing a multiparty system, strengthening the parliamentary system, restoring the Armed Forces' potential and, of course, developing the economy.

People are always teaching us democracy but the people who teach us democracy don't want to learn it themselves.

I am personally acquainted with Mr. Gates, I have met him on several occasions. I think he is a very nice man and not a bad specialist. But Mr. Gates, of course, was one of the leaders of the US Central Intelligence Agency and today he is defense secretary. If he also happens to be America's leading expert on democracy, I congratulate you.

Our country is run by the people of the Russian Federation through legitimately elected bodies of power and administration: through representative bodies (the parliament) and executive bodies (the president and the government of the Russian Federation).

Mr. McCain fought in Vietnam. I think that he has enough blood of peaceful citizens on his hands. It must be impossible for him to live without these disgusting scenes anymore.
Mr. McCain was captured and they kept him not just in prison, but in a pit for several years. Anyone in his place would go nuts.

We are not for Assad, neither for his opponents. We want to achieve the situation where the violence ends and there won't be large-scale civil war. How many of peaceful people were killed by so-called militants? Did you count? There are also hundreds of victims. What is happening in Libya, in Iraq? Did they become safer? Where are they heading? Nobody has an answer.

I'd rather not deal with such questions, because anyway it's like shearing a pig – lots of screams but little wool.

Any minority's right to be different must be re-spected, but the right of the majority must not be questioned.

Without the values at the core of Christianity and other world religions, without moral norms that have been shaped over millennia, people will inevitably lose their human dignity.

As for some countries' concerns about Russia's possible aggressive actions, I think that only an insane person and only in a dream can imagine that Russia would suddenly attack NATO. I think some countries are simply taking advantage of people's fears with regard to Russia. They just want to play the role of front-line countries that should receive some supplementary military, economic, financial or some other aid. Therefore, it is pointless to support this idea; it is absolutely groundless. But some may be interested in fostering such fears. I can only make a conjecture.

The Americans do not want Russia's rapprochement with Europe. I am not asserting this, it is just a hypothesis. Let's suppose that the United States would like to maintain its leadership in the Atlantic community. It needs an external threat, an external enemy to ensure this leadership.

Many Euro-Atlantic countries have moved away from their roots, including Christian values. Policies are being pursued that place on the same level a multi-child family and a same-sex partnership, a faith in God and a belief in Satan.

It's always hard to play a double game – to declare a fight against terrorists but at the same time try to use some of them to move the pieces on the Middle Eastern chessboard in your own favor.

I am confident that at least for the coming 25 years American missile defenses will not cause any substantial damage to the national security of Russia. But we will reinforce our capability by mounting multiple warheads on our missiles and that will cost us a meager sum. And so, the nuclear arsenal of Russia will be augmented multifold.

I am very confident that without a free media, we cannot have a normal democratic society.

Peace, a life at peace, has always been and continues to be an ideal for humanity. But peace as a state of world politics has never been stable.

In the last quarter-century, the threshold for applying force has clearly been lowered. Immunity against war, acquired as a result of two world wars literally on a psychological, subconscious level, has been weakened.

Europe's problem is that it doesn't have an independent foreign policy.

The most important thing is not to undermine legitimate governments, not to destroy their statehood even if it appears to be imperfect.

I think that no one should ever impose any values, which he/she considers to be correct, on others. We have our own values and our own ideas about justice — in all cases strictly observing inviolable international law.

I guess that political nouveaux riches have lost a sense of reality. There are some countries and nations that will never accept a secondary role, a role of an occupied country or some kind of a vassal. It will end sooner or later. Soon enough, I guess.

It is essential for future development to build relations of the so-called geopolitical struggle. The fight is inevitable and it is normal. It is only necessary to conduct it in compliance with the civilized rules.

You cannot improve anything by organizing a coup. Has anything improved in the country? The power is in the hands of oligarchs.

Attempts to promote a model of unilateral domination, as I have said on numerous occasions, have led to an imbalance in the system of international law and global regulation, which means there is a threat, and political, economic or military competition may get out of control.

Global information space is shaken by wars today. The only correct viewpoint is hegemonically imposed on others.

Authorities in countries that seemed to have always appealed to such values as freedom of speech and the free dissemination of information are now trying to prevent the spreading of objective information and any opinion that differs from their own.

There are things arguing against which is
impossible.

There is no one to talk to since Mahatma Gandhi died.

Nobody should have any illusion about the possibility of gaining military superiority over Russia. We will never allow this to happen.

The Russian army is polite, but menacing.
Impossible to defeat her.

Russia would never swing its nuclear club at others. I hope no person is insane enough on planet earth who would dare to use nuclear weapons.

Peace is humanity's ideal. War turns nations
against each other, vying for dominance.
Today's nuclear weapons assure no winner
in a global conflict.

Let me tell you something – there is no need to fear Russia. The world has changed so drastically that people with some common sense cannot even imagine such a large-scale military conflict today. We have other things to think about, I assure you.

I'm eternally grateful to fate and the citizens of Russia that they've trusted me to be the head of the Russian government. Give me twenty years, and you will not recognize Russia.

I have worked like a galley slave throughout these eight years, morning till night, and I have given all I could to this work. I am happy with the results.

For the preservation of the majestic Russia.

2015 U.N. General Assembly Speech

Your excellency Mr. President, your excellency Mr. Secretary General, distinguished heads of state and government, ladies and gentlemen, the 70th anniversary of the United Nations is a good occasion to both take stock of history and talk about our common future.

In 1945, the countries that defeated Nazism joined their efforts to lay solid foundations for the postwar world order. But I remind you that the key decisions on the principles guiding the cooperation among states, as well as on the establishment of the United Nations, were made in our country, in Yalta, at the meeting of the anti-Hitler coalition leaders.

The Yalta system was actually born in travail. It was won at the cost of tens of millions of lives and two world wars. This swept through the planet in the 20th century. Let us be fair. It helped humanity through turbulent, at times dramatic, events of the last seven decades. It saved the world from large-scale upheavals.

The United Nations is unique in its legitimacy, representation and universality. It is true that lately the U.N. has been widely criticized for supposedly not being efficient enough, and for the fact that the decision-making on fundamental issues stalls due to insurmountable differences, first of all, among the members of the Security Council.

However, I'd like to point out there have always been differences in the U.N. throughout all these 70 years of existence. The veto right has always been exercised by the United States, the United Kingdom, France, China, the Soviet Union and Russia later, alike. It is absolutely natural for so diverse and representative an organization.

When the U.N. was established, its founders did not in the least think that there would always be unanimity. The mission of the organization is to seek and reach compromises, and its strength comes from taking different views and opinions into consideration. Decisions debated within the U.N. are either taken as resolutions or not. As diplomats say, they either pass or do not pass.

Whatever actions any state might take bypassing this procedure are illegitimate. They run counter to the charter and defy international law. We all know that after the end of the Cold War — everyone is aware of that — a single center of domination emerged in the world, and then those who found themselves at the top of the pyramid were tempted to think that if they were strong and exceptional, they knew better and they did not have to reckon with the U.N., which, instead of [acting to] automatically authorize and legitimize the necessary decisions, often creates obstacles or, in other words, stands in the way.

It has now become commonplace to see that in its original form, it has become obsolete and completed its historical mission. Of course, the world is changing and the U.N. must be consistent with this natural transformation. Russia stands ready to work together with its partners on the basis of full consensus, but we consider the attempts to undermine the legitimacy of the United Nations as extremely dangerous. They could lead to a collapse of the entire architecture of international organizations, and then indeed there would be no other rules left but the rule of force.

We would get a world dominated by selfishness rather than collective work, a world increasingly characterized by dictate rather than equality. There would be less of a chain of democracy and freedom, and that would be a world where true independent states would be replaced by an ever-growing number of de facto protectorates and externally controlled territories.

What is the state sovereignty, after all, that has been mentioned by our colleagues here? It is basically about freedom and the right to choose freely one's own future for every person, nation and state. By the way, dear colleagues, the same holds true of the question of the so-called legitimacy of state authority. One should not play with or manipulate words.

Every term in international law and international affairs should be clear, transparent and have uniformly understood criteria. We are all different, and we should respect that. No one has to conform to a single development model that someone has once and for all recognized as the only right one. We should all remember what our past has taught us.

We also remember certain episodes from the history of the Soviet Union. Social experiments for export, attempts to push for changes within other countries based on ideological preferences, often led to tragic consequences and to degradation rather than progress.

It seemed, however, that far from learning from others' mistakes, everyone just keeps repeating them, and so the export of revolutions, this time of so-called democratic ones, continues. It would suffice to look at the situation in the Middle East and North Africa, as has been mentioned by previous speakers. Certainly political and social problems in this region have been piling up for a long time, and people there wish for changes naturally.

But how did it actually turn out? Rather than bringing about reforms, an aggressive foreign interference has resulted in a brazen destruction of national institutions and the lifestyle itself. Instead of the triumph of democracy and progress, we got violence, poverty and social disaster. Nobody cares a bit about human rights, including the right to life.

I cannot help asking those who have caused the situation, do you realize now what you've done? But I am afraid no one is going to answer that. Indeed, policies based on self-conceit and belief in one's exceptionality and impunity have never been abandoned.

It is now obvious that the power vacuum created in some countries of the Middle East and North Africa through the emergence of anarchy areas, which immediately started to be filled with extremists and terrorists.

Tens of thousands of militants are fighting under the banners of the so-called Islamic State. Its ranks include former Iraqi servicemen who were thrown out into the street after the invasion of Iraq in 2003. Many recruits also come from Libya, a country whose statehood was destroyed as a result of a gross violation of the U.N. Security Council Resolution 1973. And now, the ranks of radicals are being joined by the members of the so-called moderate Syrian opposition supported by the Western countries.

First, they are armed and trained and then they defect to the so-called Islamic State. Besides, the Islamic State itself did not just come from nowhere. It was also initially forged as a tool against undesirable secular regimes.

Having established a foothold in Iraq and Syria, the Islamic State has begun actively expanding to other regions. It is seeking dominance in the Islamic world. And not only there, and its plans go further than that. The situation is more than dangerous.

In these circumstances, it is hypocritical and irresponsible to make loud declarations about the threat of international terrorism while turning a blind eye to the channels of financing and supporting terrorists, including the process of trafficking and illicit trade in oil and arms. It would be equally irresponsible to try to manipulate extremist groups and place them at one's service in order to achieve one's own political goals in the hope of later dealing with them or, in other words, liquidating them.

To those who do so, I would like to say — dear sirs, no doubt you are dealing with rough and cruel people, but they're in no way primitive or silly. They are just as clever as you are, and you never know who is manipulating whom. And the recent data on arms transferred to this most moderate opposition is the best proof of it.

We believe that any attempts to play games with terrorists, let alone to arm them, are not just short-sighted, but fire hazardous. This may result in the global terrorist threat increasing dramatically and engulfing new regions, especially given that Islamic State camps train militants from many countries, including the European countries.

Unfortunately, dear colleagues, I have to put it frankly: Russia is not an exception. We cannot allow these criminals who already tasted blood to return back home and continue their evil doings. No one wants this to happen, does he?

Russia has always been consistently fighting against terrorism in all its forms. Today, we provide military and technical assistance both to Iraq and Syria and many other countries of the region who are fighting terrorist groups.

We think it is an enormous mistake to refuse to cooperate with the Syrian government and its armed forces, who are valiantly fighting terrorism face to face. We should finally acknowledge that no one but President Assad's armed forces and Kurds militias are truly fighting the Islamic State and other terrorist organizations in Syria.

We know about all the problems and contradictions in the region, but which were based on the reality.

Dear colleagues, I must note that such an honest and frank approach of Russia has been recently used as a pretext to accuse it of its growing ambitions, as if those who say it have no ambitions at all.

However, it's not about Russia's ambitions, dear colleagues, but about the recognition of the fact that we can no longer tolerate the current state of affairs in the world. What we actually propose is to be guided by common values and common interests, rather than ambitions.

On the basis of international law, we must join efforts to address the problems that all of us are facing and create a genuinely broad international coalition against terrorism.

Similar to the anti-Hitler coalition, it could unite a broad range of forces that are resolutely resisting those who, just like the Nazis, sow evil and hatred of humankind. And, naturally, the Muslim countries are to play a key role in the coalition, even more so because the Islamic State does not only pose a direct threat to them, but also desecrates one of the greatest world religions by its bloody crimes.

The ideologists of militants make a mockery of Islam and pervert its true humanistic values. I would like to address Muslim spiritual leaders, as well. Your authority and your guidance are of great importance right now.

It is essential to prevent people recruited by militants from making hasty decisions and those who have already been deceived, and who, due to various circumstances found themselves among terrorists, need help in finding a way back to normal life, laying down arms, and putting an end to fratricide.

Russia will shortly convene, as the current president of the Security Council, a ministerial meeting to carry out a comprehensive analysis of threats in the Middle East.

First of all, we propose discussing whether it is possible to agree on a resolution aimed at coordinating the actions of all the forces that confront the Islamic State and other terrorist organizations. Once again, this coordination should be based on the principles of the U.N. Charter.

We hope that the international community will be able to develop a comprehensive strategy of political stabilization, as well as social and economic recovery, of the Middle East. Then, dear friends, there would be no need for new refugee camps. Today, the flow of people who were forced to leave their homeland has literally engulfed first neighboring countries and then Europe itself. There were hundreds of thousands of them now, and there might be millions before long.

In fact, it is a new great and tragic migration of peoples, and it is a harsh lesson for all of us, including Europe.

I would like to stress refugees undoubtedly need our compassion and support. However, the — on the way to solve this problem at a fundamental level is to restore their statehood where it has been destroyed, to strengthen the government institutions where they still exist or are being reestablished, to provide comprehensive assistance of military, economic and material nature to countries in a difficult situation. And certainly, to those people who, despite all the ordeals, will not abandon their homes. Literally, any assistance to sovereign states can and must be offered rather than imposed exclusively and solely in accordance with the U.N. Charter.

In other words, everything in this field that has been done or will be done pursuant to the norms of international law must be supported by our organization. Everything that contravenes the U.N. Charter must be rejected. Above all, I believe it is of the utmost importance to help restore government's institutions in Libya, support the new government of Iraq and provide comprehensive assistance to the legitimate government of Syria.

Dear colleagues, ensuring peace and regional and global stability remains the key objective of the international community with the U.N. at its helm. We believe this means creating a space of equal and indivisible security, which is not for the select few but for everyone. Yet, it is a challenge and complicated and time-consuming task, but there is simply no other alternative. However, the bloc thinking of the times of the Cold War and the desire to explore new geopolitical areas is still present among some of our colleagues.

First, they continue their policy of expanding NATO. What for? If the Warsaw Bloc stopped its existence, the Soviet Union collapsed and, nevertheless, the NATO continues expanding as well as its military infrastructure. Then they offered the poor Soviet countries a false choice: either to be with the West or with the East. Sooner or later, this logic of confrontation was bound to spark off a grave geopolitical crisis. This is exactly what happened in Ukraine, where the discontent of population with the current authorities was used and the military coup was orchestrated from outside — that triggered a civil war as a result.

We're confident that only through full and faithful implementation of the Minsk agreements of February 12th, 2015, can we put an end to the bloodshed and find a way out of the deadlock. Ukraine's territorial integrity cannot be ensured by threat of force and force of arms. What is needed is a genuine consideration for the interests and rights of the people in the Donbas region and respect for their choice. There is a need to coordinate with them as provided for by the Minsk agreements, the key elements of the country's political structure. These steps will guarantee that Ukraine will develop as a civilized society, as an essential link and building a common space of security and economic cooperation, both in Europe and in Eurasia.

Ladies and gentlemen, I have mentioned these common space of economic cooperation on purpose. Not long ago, it seemed that in the economic sphere, with its objective market loss, we would launch a leaf without dividing lines. We would build on transparent and jointly formulated rules, including the WTO principles, stipulating the freedom of trade, and investment and open competition.

Nevertheless, today, unilateral sanctions circumventing the U.N. Charter have become commonplace, in addition to pursuing political objectives. The sanctions serve as a means of eliminating competitors.

I would like to point out another sign of a growing economic selfishness. Some countries [have] chosen to create closed economic associations, with the establishment being negotiated behind the scenes, in secret from those countries' own citizens, the general public, business community and from other countries.

Other states whose interests may be affected are not informed of anything, either. It seems that we are about to be faced with an accomplished fact that the rules of the game have been changed in favor of a narrow group of the privileged, with the WTO having no say. This could unbalance the trade system completely and disintegrate the global economic space.

These issues affect the interest of all states and influence the future of the world economy as a whole. That is why we propose discussing them within the U.N. WTO NGO (ph) '20. Contrary to the policy of exclusiveness, Russia proposes harmonizing original economic projects. I refer to the so-called integration of integrations based on universal and transparent rules of international trade. As an example, I would like to cite our plans to interconnect the Eurasian economic union, and China's initiative of the Silk Road economic belt.

We still believe that harmonizing the integration processes within the Eurasian Economic Union and the European Union is highly promising.

Ladies and gentlemen, the issues that affect the future of all people include the challenge of global climate change. It is in our interest to make the U.N. Climate Change Conference to be held in December in Paris a success.

As part of our national contribution, we plan to reduce by 2030 the greenhouse emissions to 70, 75 percent of the 1990 level.

I suggest, however, we should take a wider view on this issue. Yes, we might defuse the problem for a while, by setting quotas on harmful emissions or by taking other measures that are nothing but tactical. But we will not solve it that way. We need a completely different approach.

We have to focus on introducing fundamental and new

technologies inspired by nature, which would not damage the environment, but would be in harmony with it. Also, that would allow us to restore the balance upset by biosphere and technosphere upset by human activities.

It is indeed a challenge of planetary scope, but I'm confident that humankind has intellectual potential to address it. We need to join our efforts. I refer, first of all, to the states that have a solid research basis and have made significant advances in fundamental science.

We propose convening a special forum under the U.N. auspices for a comprehensive consideration of the issues related to the depletion of natural resources, destruction of habitat and climate change.

Russia would be ready to co-sponsor such a forum.

Ladies and gentlemen, colleagues, it was on the 10th of January, 1946, in London that the U.N. General Assembly gathered for its first session.

Mr. Suleta, a Colombian diplomat and the chairman of the Preparatory Commission, opened the session by giving, I believe, a concise definition of the basic principles that the U.N. should follow in its activities, which are free will, defiance of scheming and trickery and spirit of cooperation.

Today, his words sound as a guidance for all of us. Russia believes in the huge potential of the United Nations, which should help us avoid a new global confrontation and engage in strategic cooperation. Together with other countries, we will consistently work towards strengthening the central coordinating role of the U.N. I'm confident that by working together, we will make the world stable and safe, as well as provide conditions for the development of all states and nations.

Thank you.

COPYRIGHT NOTICE

Made in the USA
Lexington, KY
15 April 2018